MARDI GRAS TREASURES

COSTUME DESIGNS OF THE GOLDEN AGE

MARDI GRAS TREASURES
COSTUME DESIGNS OF THE GOLDEN AGE

Henri Schindler

PELICAN PUBLISHING COMPANY
Gretna 2002

To Tina Freeman

*The word "Pelican" and the depiction of a pelican are trademarks
of Pelican Publishing Company, Inc., and are registered
in the U.S. Patent and Trademark Office.*

Library of Congress Cataloging-in-Publication Data

Schindler, Henri.
  Mardi Gras treasures : costume designs of the Golden Age / Henri
Schindler.
      p. cm.
Includes index.
  ISBN 1-56554-724-1 (alk. paper)
  1. Carnival costume—Louisiana—New Orleans I. Title.
GT4211.N4 S369 2002
391'.009763'35—dc21
                                        2002004752

Page 1: *Anon., "Female Eye," water-color costume design for Comus pag-
    eant, 1869: "The Five Senses." (The earliest surviving costume designs
    of the New Orleans Carnival, the male and female eyes appeared among
    the characters on the second float, "Sight.")*
Page 2: *Ceneilla Alexander, "Page," water-color costume design for Rex
    page, circa 1923.*
Page 3: *Charles Briton, "Sea Dragon," water-color costume design for the
    Comus pageant, 1873: "The Missing Links to Darwin's Origin of
    Species."*
Page 5: *Anon., "Male Eye," water-color costume design for Comus pag-
    eant, 1869: "The Five Senses."*
Page 6: *Ceneilla Alexander, "Plate No. 1," water-color costume design for
    Rex, King of the Carnival, circa 1925.*

Printed in Korea
Published by Pelican Publishing Company, Inc.
1000 Burmaster Street, Gretna, Louisiana 70053

CONTENTS

Rhine stone
tassels →

INTRODUCTION

The exuberant theatricality that has long distinguished New Orleans found its first expression in the costumes and masks of Mardi Gras. Decades before the first Creole cavalcade or stately pageant, masquerade balls were the most popular entertainment of the New Orleans Carnival. Beginning around 1800, costumed revelers of every station filled the public dance halls, elegant theaters, and hotel ballrooms. The carefree, parade-like traffic to these numerous balls drew hundreds of maskers to the narrow streets of the old Creole sector. Benjamin Latrobe, who later designed the United States Capitol, wrote in *Appearance of New Orleans in 1819*: "As it is now the Carnival, every evening is closed with a ball, a play, or a concert." The Carnival season culminated with Mardi Gras, which brought forth the greatest parade of costumes and masks. There was regalia from every nation and epoch, an array of grotesque, quizzical, diabolical, horrible, strange masks, and disguises, of demigods and demi-beasts, apes and man-bats from the moon, joined by mermaids and Punchinellos, by satyrs prancing with monks, and savages dancing with shepherd girls and nuns.

Cross-dressing was not merely tolerated during Carnival, it was applauded—and widespread. Behind their Mardi Gras disguises, both sexes impersonated one another, with exaggerated costuming and theatrical mimicry. On Gallatin Street, the raucous sailor district, most of the women were dressed as men and the men as women. Several newspapers reported the costume and mien of a masker on Canal Street: "One we noticed as particularly good. It seemed to be a boy of about sixteen, with a female cast of countenance, who was rigged up in fashionable female attire. The skirts of his, or her dress, were hooped out so extravagantly that the whole sidewalk was covered, and the bonnet was so wonderfully small it covered but a portion of the back of the head, leaving a flood of ringlets free to flutter as they pleased."

The frequent indulgence of cross-dressing for Mardi Gras was equaled or surpassed only by the popularity of transracial masking. The *Tribune*, a French-language newspaper published by Creoles of color, noted in 1867: "Strangers who have never seen a masquerade in New Orleans must be struck by the large number of people who mask as Negro characters." Almost all of Carnival's full-face masks came from France. With androgynous features painted in tones of cream and pink, these masks were sold throughout the city and were worn by numerous African-American revelers. Every Mardi Gras brought white maskers who changed both race and gender: men costumed as black mammies, and women as minstrels or tramps.

Rooted in antiquity, this pervasive devotion to costumes and masks remained as essential to the New Orleans Carnival as it was to the carnivals of ancient Greece, imperial Rome, or medieval France. In *Games and Mankind,* French philosopher Roger Caillois wrote: "Mankind has always known the mask. This enigmatic and seemingly useless accessory is more common than the lever, bow and arrow, spear or plough. No tool, no invention, belief, custom or institution lends such a degree of unity to mankind as does the mask. Entire peoples, while ignoring the most basic and precious utensils, have known the mask. Whole civilizations have prospered without any notion of the wheel or its potential applications, yet to them the mask was familiar."

Beginning in early childhood, natives of New Orleans were introduced to the magic of masks and costumes. Each generation brought new participants and fresh disguises to the festival, but the joyous spirit of Carnival went unchanged. For the costumes and play of Mardi Gras were not merely traditions; they were ingrained in the city's psyche. This *Picayune* editorial of 1912 would have been as accurate a century earlier as it will likely be decades from today: "By far the most interesting feature of Mardi Gras is the parading of promiscuous maskers all over the city. Singly or in groups these merrymakers affect almost every grotesque or fanciful character imaginable, and their antics provide the real fun of the culminating day of the Carnival."

While the palpable, irreducible joy of Mardi Gras lay in its mingling sea of masked humanity, even larger crowds gathered annually to witness the series of brilliant pageants with masks and costumes of another order. The first thematic procession was staged by the Mistick Krewe of Comus on Mardi Gras night in 1857. On that triumphant evening, with two floats and a marching host of richly costumed devils depicting "The Demon Actors in Milton's *Paradise Lost*," Comus introduced rolling theatrical spectacles to the streets of New Orleans. The wealthy young founders of the Mistick Krewe chose as their leader the demigod sorcerer of John Milton's "Comus," a masque first performed at Ludlow Castle, Wales, in 1634.

The scenic pageantry of Carnival was a belated descendant of masques, the lavishly mounted theatricals that were popular among the aristocracies of sixteenth- and seventeenth-century Europe. Kings, princes, nobles, and their ladies reenacted the classic Greek myths with song, dance, and opulent costuming. These entertainments were most frequently performed in intimate palace theaters, but for momentous occasions, like a royal wedding, they were moved outdoors, where they were staged before a multitude, and often culminated with fabulous displays of pyrotechnics.

Another, more humble ancestor must be acknowledged. Michael Krafft was born in Bristol, Pennsylvania, around 1807 and moved to Mobile, Alabama, in his early youth. Mobile had known night parades since 1798, when the Spanish Mystic Society marched on Twelfth Night. In 1830, when he was only twenty-three years old, Krafft was the moving spirit in founding the Cowbellion de Rakin Society. The New Year's Day parades of the Mummers in Philadelphia may have influenced Krafft, for the Cowbellions made their appearances on New Year's Eve.

For their first ten years, the Cowbellions moved on foot through the streets of Mobile, with a few small floats decorated with transparencies and paintings on forms made of glass or thin cloth, and illuminated from within. In 1840 they presented their first tableau pageant based on mythological themes, "Heathen Gods and Goddesses." On New Year's Eve of 1856, the Cowbellions offered "Pandemonium Unveiled"; six weeks later, on Mardi

Gras night, the costumes and masks from "Pandemonium" were worn by the devils in the first Comus parade. (The costumes and masks were borrowed by Comus and used in this first New Orleans thematic procession.) In Perry Young's magisterial history of Carnival, *The Mistick Krewe*, Krafft is lauded as the father of Mardi Gras pageantry: "His mystic progeny are legion. [The parades] are copies, not of a Carnival which once held sway in Italy or France, but of a pageantry initiated by Krafft and his gay fellows, and deftly fitted into the ancient Carnival at New Orleans by an evolution of its own."

In this artistic evolution of New Orleans Mardi Gras, the Golden Age began in the early 1870s, with the pageants and tableau balls of Twelfth Night Revelers, Rex, and the Knights of Momus. It then blossomed in the 1880s with the Krewe of Proteus, reached its zenith in the 1890s and early 1900s, and endured until the onset of the Great Depression in 1930. This book, the third in a series of *Mardi Gras Treasures*, presents the first comprehensive survey of the wondrous costumes designed for the casts in the papier-mâché tableaux of Golden Age parades and balls.

These glorious productions recreated scenes from classical mythology, history, literature, religion, nature, and whimsy. One hundred or more costumes were designed for the krewe members who rode the floats; these riding members were referred to as "the cast" and each of them was assigned a number. Number One was the member who was chosen each year to lead the parade as Comus, Momus, or Proteus. Cast members from numbers 2 through 100 were masked and clad to impersonate a staggering array of characters, attired in costumes constructed to their individual measurements. Cross-dressing was essential in all of the pageants and balls. Every female character was brought to life by an all-male cast; no matter how delicate or feminine some costumes may appear, they were worn with delight by generations of the most prominent businessmen in New Orleans.

For fifty years or more, these fantasy wardrobes were made in Paris, the capital of style and workmanship. The New Orleans artists who created these water-color costume plates also designed the floats, ball invitations, and court jewels. (The reader seeking biographical material on the artists is advised to see the preceding volume in this series, *Float Designs of the Golden Age*.) The works in this volume have been organized by artist, and are presented chronologically. One of this author's greatest pleasures in researching collections of Mardi Gras material has been the discovery and identification of hitherto unidentified early designs, such as the two costume plates by an anonymous artist for the Comus parade of 1869, "The Five Senses." As these designs and hundreds of other Mardi Gras treasures emerge from a century or more of oblivion to be appreciated by new generations, we continue to dream of the wonders that yet lie hidden.

MARDI GRAS TREASURES
COSTUME DESIGNS OF THE GOLDEN AGE

Charles Briton, "Louisiana—Her Founders and Defenders," water-color design of ensemble tableau for Comus Ball of 1870, "The History of Louisiana."

CHAPTER I

CHARLES BRITON

There is scant visual record of early Comus parades. From the first ten years, we have only a preliminary float design for 1858 and engravings from 1858 and 1867. Two costume plates from the 1867 "Triumph of Epicurus" were reproduced in Perry Young's 1931 Carnival history, *The Mistick Krewe,* but the album of designs has since disappeared. We are left to contemplate the written descriptions of wonders, such as this one concerning the Comus float in 1857's "Demon Actors": "Satan high on a hill, far blazing as a mount, with pyramids and towers from diamond quarries hewn, and rocks of gold."

The papier-mâché figures and décor for the small floats were made in Paris, as were the krewe costumes, but no mention survived of the artist or artists who designed 1869 Comus production, "The Five Senses." However, a water-color and gouache rendering of the ensemble tableau of the 1870 Comus ball, "The History of Louisiana,"

was painted by Charles Briton, beginning Carnival's earliest-known designing career.

Cast members in the 1870 tableau portrayed the early explorers, founders, statesmen, and dignitaries of Creole Louisiana together with her daughter, New Orleans; her wealth, cotton, sugar, and rice; and Miche Sepe (Mississippi, Father of Waters). All of these characters were painted to resemble marble statues, as they had appeared earlier in the sixteen-float parade, posing motionless atop granite blocks. Together with the fleeting joys and ritual solemnities attending the Mistick Krewe, this celebration of pre-American Louisiana also offered an unequivocal testament to the cultural alchemy that was taking place in New Orleans.

Comus had employed marble statuary ten years earlier in his 1860 pageant, "Statues of the Great Men of Our Country." At that time, the long-standing cultural antagonism between the brash, nouveaux riche Americans and the old Creole society was still palpable, and the Creole press scorned the Comus parade: "The various [American] characters are not worth a description, either for who they were or for the uptown citizens concealed behind them." A decade later, in the years following the Civil War, as the longer-lasting strife of Reconstruction settled over New Orleans, the enmity between uptown Americans and downtown Creoles was largely forgotten.

The city's Anglo-Saxon population, resident for three generations and ascendant for two, found themselves closer to the Creoles than to their former brethren in the North. Uptown residents shared the Creole hostility to the new wave of American adventurers they both called "carpetbaggers." The Golden Age of Carnival began in the troubled days of Reconstruction. With the advent of new societies and glittering courts, Mardi Gras became much more than a beloved festival—it became a fantastic empire, a wonderland of wealth and grandeur, the counterkingdom in which the worldly old city still reigned.

As each of the new krewes joined the Carnival pantheon, they turned to Charles Briton for their designs. Because of the transitory nature of the scenes to which they gave form, perhaps Briton's designs were later discarded like obsolete blueprints. Whatever combination of carelessness or misfortune followed their completion, only a few collections of his extraordinary designs for the principal pageants of the 1870s and early 1880s have survived. Twelfth Night Revelers, formalizing the old Creole calendar of Carnival, made their first appearance on January 6, 1870, with a torch-lit procession, followed by a tableau ball. Briton's designs for the Twelfth Night procession of 1871, "Mother Goose's Tea Party," are the earliest complete set of parade watercolors.

Briton's draftsmanship animates the march with comedic robustness and physical grace. Everything seems vibrant and alive and the panorama seems to be in motion, as it was on that now-distant night, but whatever satire accompanied the "Mother Goose" parade is lost to us today.

Two years later, as Reconstruction tensions increased and two companies of soldiers were called to reinforce federal troops occupying New Orleans, the Carnival season of 1873 was opened with the Twelfth Night Revelers production, "The World of Audubon." The Audubon pageant, an apparent tribute to the great naturalist and former New Orleans resident, was remembered years later as one among the finest of all Carnival creations, by virtue of its costumes. The Parrot, Pelican, Kingfisher, Ibis, Flamingo, Owl, Cardinal, Vulture, and others were all wrought in endless layers of Parisian silks and velvet. This fabulous avian cast, so pleasing to the eye, enacted a series of pointed tableaux, among them "Political Barnyard Meeting," with Fox addressing Fowls; and "The Pelican," the insignia of the seal of Louisiana, feeding her three fledglings, who kept falling from the nest. Briton's watercolor of the ensemble tableau is the only surviving remnant of the legendary costumes.

Carnival of 1873 began with a stunning satire and was closed seven weeks later when the Mistick Krewe of Comus presented the masterpiece of the genre, "The Missing Links to Darwin's Origin of Species." The order of march followed the stanzas of an ingenious poem written by E. C. Hancock, a New Orleans newspaper editor and prominent member of Comus; each stanza was borne aloft on gaslit transparencies, in a succession of verse that traced the evolution of life from Sponge to Gorilla. The Mistick Krewe were all afoot, inside one hundred wondrous papier-mâché animals, fish, flowers, insects, and sea creatures, some of them twelve feet high. And as the Darwinian march unfolded in the glare of torches, many of the Missing Links bore unmistakable resemblance to political figures of the day, from local precincts to the White House.

The remarkable invention and malevolent wit of "The Missing Links" secured its position among the greatest efforts of New Orleans Carnival, but Briton's water-color designs were not seen at the time. Hancock's poem was printed as the ball program and illustrated with pen-and-ink drawings of the characters in each biological group. An engraving depicting the final tableau of the ball appeared a few months later in *Harper's* magazine, while other ball scenes and a number of Links were included in B. M. Comfrey's delightful New Orleans illustrations for *Scribner's*.

Only scattered handfuls of Briton's designs for Rex or Momus have survived, the earliest being two water-color plates from the fourth Rex parade, reflecting the broad theme chosen for 1876, "Persian and Egyptian." In the waning days of Reconstruction, Momus unleashed the most vitriolic parade in Carnival history, "Hades—A Dream of Momus." Briton's float designs for the legendary Momus pageant of 1877 were recorded in a small black-and-white lithograph, the costumes in a large watercolor depicting the ensemble tableau of the ball.

The furor that erupted over "Hades" had subsided five days later. On Mardi Gras morning, Rex appeared as Charlemagne, riding with twelve peers in armor and accompanied by a royal guard, presenting "Military Progress of the World." Briton's beautifully painted costume plates, many of them boasting extraordinary detail, were collected and bound by the gentleman who reigned that year as Rex, Charles T. Howard, and presented to his daughter.

Briton romped effortlessly from classic myth to popular travesty, sometimes combining them as he did with the comic presentations of Rex's, "The Gods Modernized" (1878), "History of the World" (1879), and "The Four Elements" (1880). The Carnival of 1880 also featured one of Comus's most impressive historical displays, "The Aztec People and Their Conquest by Cortez," as well as the widely criticized Momus effort, "A Dream of Fair Women." Society writer Catherine Cole complained: "They attempted to portray 'A Dream of Fair Women,' but I confess my imagination was not vivid enough to fancy 'fair women' in the lot of gorgeously appareled brawny men who hid their beards and moustaches behind false faces. Adieu! It was a perfect nightmare."

Rex's subject for 1882 was "The Pursuit of Pleasure," with two floats depicting Mardi Gras: "The Pleasures of Mardi Gras—Morning" and "The Pleasures of Mardi Gras—Evening." Briton's design for the "Morning" float presented a deeply wrinkled older gentleman of sour countenance, gowned and winged, preparing to don a beautiful mask, completing his transformation into a golden-haired fairy. On the "Evening" float, a group of maskers were depicted backstage, receiving instructions for the coming tableau. All of the characters—Death, a fire demon, Mother Goose, a high priest and priestess, and Medusa—were elaborately costumed and in the process of removing their masks. The high priestess was revealed as a gentleman with an extravagant moustache, and Medusa had a beard.

Between 1882 and 1884, the last three years of his life, Briton produced an astonishing volume of extraordinary design: for Rex, "The Pursuit of Pleasure," "Atlantis—the Antediluvian Kingdom," and "The Semitic Races"; for Comus, "Worships of the World" and "Illustrated Ireland"; for Momus, "The Ramayama," "The Moors in Spain," and "The Passions"; and for the first three Proteus pageants, "Ancient Egyptian Theology," "History of France," and "The Aeneid."

Briton's float plates for the first three Proteus pageants, together with his costume designs for "Ancient Egyptian Theology," are all that survive of his mature work. The exaggerated profiles, ruddy cheeks, and bulbous red noses, hallmarks of Briton's comic work, were rarely seen on the gods, heroes, or historical characters in his loftier tableaux. For the Proteus recreation of ancient Egypt, Briton designed an unsurpassed architectural display, with papier-mâché temples, tombs, palaces, and pleasure gardens, in which the gods and goddesses appeared with strange animal heads and solar discs, with serpent-headed attendants and white-robed priests. The pageant concluded with a startling scenic depiction of "Resurrection," in which an enormous phoenix, whose multihued wings spanned thirty feet, rose above the glowing coals of its parents' ashes.

In the Rex parade of the following morning, "The Pursuit of Pleasure," the playful draftsmanship, whimsical costumes, and lively gestures of Briton's humorous designs appeared for the last time. Rex preferred to illustrate the glories of lost Atlantis, and Proteus chose "The Aeneid," with its blazing "Palace of Pluto" and fabulous "Gate of Ivory." As his career of fourteen years neared its end, Briton had become Carnival's first architect, presiding over the artistic evolution of the pageants, from marching casts and a few small floats to ambitious scenes of epic grandeur.

Charles Briton, "Alligator," water-color costume design for papier-mâché walking figure in Comus pageant, 1873: "The Missing Links to Darwin's Origin of Species."

Charles Briton, water-color design for costumes and papier-mâché figures in Twelfth Night Revelers pageant, 1871: "Mother Goose's Tea Party."

Charles Briton, "Mermaid," water-color costume design for papier-mâché walking figure in Comus pageant, 1873: "The Missing Links to Darwin's Origin of Species."

Charles Briton, water-color design for costumes and papier-mâché figures in Twelfth Night Revelers pageant, 1871: "Mother Goose's Tea Party."

"Tiger."

"Lion."

"Chameleon."

"Tadpole."

"African Elephant."

"Polar Bear."

"Rhinoceros."

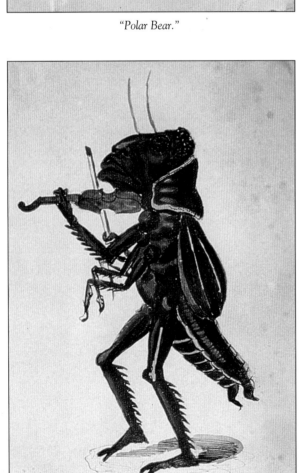

"Grasshopper."

"Gorilla."

*Charles Briton, "Musician," water-color costume
design for Rex pageant, circa 1876.*

*Charles Briton, "Umbrella Bearer," water-color
design for Rex pageant, circa 1876.*

*Charles Briton, "Caparison for Horse," water-color design for Rex
pageant, 1877: "Military Progress of the World."*

Charles Briton, "Charlemagne," water-color costume design for Rex pageant, 1877: "Military Progress of the World." (Charles T. Howard was Rex and he appeared in this costume. Briton's costume plates were beautifully bound and presented to Mr. Howard's daughter, Annie, as a memento of the occasion.)

"Queen."

IMPERIAL CROWN
OF
CHARLEMAGNE

"Pope."

"Page."

"Fool."

Charles Briton, "Pan," water-color costume design for Rex pageant, 1878: "The Gods Modernized."

Charles Briton, "Jupiter Tonans," water-color costume design for Rex pageant, 1878: "The Gods Modernized."

Charles Briton, "No. 137, The Pleasure of Mardi Gras-Morning," water-color costume design for Rex pageant, 1882: "The Pursuit of Pleasure."

Charles Briton, "No. 145, The Pleasure of Mardi Gras-Evening," water-color costume design for Rex pageant, 1882: "The Pursuit of Pleasure."

Charles Briton, "The Pleasure of Mardi Gras Evening," water-color float design for Rex pageant, 1882: "The Pursuit of Pleasure." (The cast number of each masker on the float is noted in pencil at the bottom of the design.)

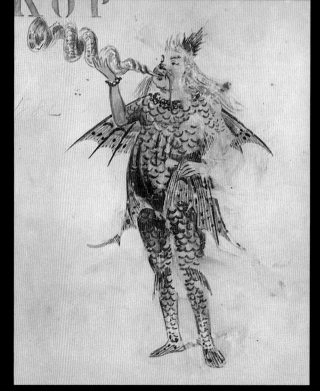

Charles Briton, "Herald," water-color costume design for attendant to Proteus in the krewe's inaugural pageant, 1882: "Ancient Egyptian Theology."

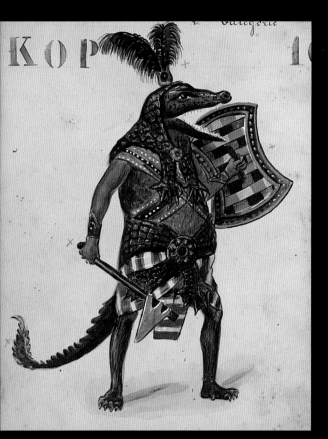

"Typhon."

Charles Briton, "Warrior of Typhon," water-color costume design for Proteus pageant, 1882: "Ancient Egyptian Theology."

Ammon Kneph (The letters "KOP" stand for "Krewe of Proteus." The float design, "Innundation of the Nile," appears on page 28 in Float Designs of the Golden Age.)

"High Priest."

"Cnoupis."

"Anubis." (Float design, "Sacred Animals," appears on page 27 in Float Designs of the Golden Age.)

Charles Briton, "Horus," water-color costume design for
Proteus pageant, 1882: "Ancient Egyptian Theology."

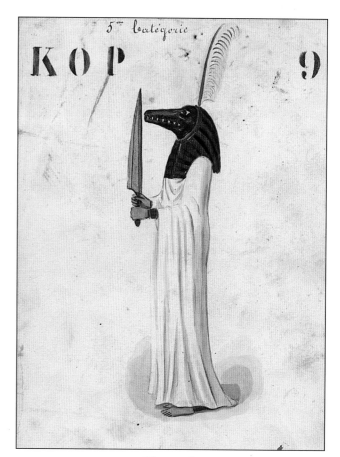

"Warrior of Horus."

"Priest of Pubastis."

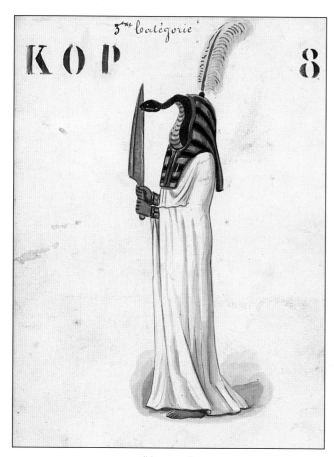

"Assessor."

"Assessor."

Charles Briton, "Pasht," water-color costume design for
Proteus pageant, 1882: "Ancient Egyptian Theology."

CHAPTER II

CARLOTTA BONNECAZE

In celebration of its centennial in 1981, the Krewe of Proteus commissioned noted New Orleans historian Charles L. Dufour to document its colorful history. Dozens of hitherto unpublished photographs and illustrations appeared in *Krewe of Proteus—The First Hundred Years*, among them several preliminary float drawings and finished water-color float plates. Attribution of these designs to Carlotta Bonnecaze seemed to solve a great Carnival mystery, one that had intrigued this writer for years: the identity of the Proteus designer who succeeded Charles Briton in 1885 and worked until the late 1890s.

The preliminary float designs—some in pencil, others in pen and ink—were given to the Louisiana State Museum in 1922 and identified as the work of Carlotta Bonnecaze, the source for Dufour's credit. The only other documentation that Carlotta Bonnecaze ever existed is a pamphlet from a 1934 exhibition of Carnival art, identifying her as the designer for Proteus. The name—Carlotta Bonnecaze—could hardly be more exotic. Worldly and faintly decadent, eccentric, and theatrical, it is a name Lafcadio Hearn might have created for the heroine of a New Orleans tale of splendidly overgrown ruins and Creole ghosts. This writer's search of twenty years has produced no further record—the life of Carlotta Bonnecaze remains shrouded in mystery.

Meanwhile, we have an extraordinary body of work to contemplate. Nearly one thousand Proteus costume plates designed between 1885 and 1897 have survived, forming the largest collection of Carnival art by one artist—work that should remain, for now, attributed to Bonnecaze. Greek mythology, the frequent subject of Carnival pageants, was never investigated by Bonnecaze. She preferred to draw from the myths of the East or Scandinavia, or create whimsical visions of the natural world, producing designs often stamped with her unique romantic strangeness and zany good humor.

Her debut in 1885, "Myths and Worships of the Chinese," was also aglow with opulently jeweled walls and vaulted ceilings of precious metals, gardens of bejeweled palm trees and golden vines, and other scenes of heavenly splendor. Proteus, richly costumed in robes of imperial yellow, represented Tien-Dze, the Sun of Heaven. Next came Pouan-Kou, the first man, in his quaint costume of leaves, followed by cast members dressed and masked as gods, sages, demons, celestial attendants, and lamas. In the costumes for the final tableau, "Giehva," or Chinese hell, we first encounter the theatrical stylistic touches that continued to distinguish her work. The maskers, clad in body stockings and wrapped in brief skirts of flame, stamped their feet and flailed their arms in beautifully choreographed gestures of anguish, one with flames pouring from his mouth, another from his topknot.

In the following year, 1886, Bonnecaze called forth one of her finest works, "Visions of Other Worlds." Golden salamanders stood upright, dancing beneath molten waves of flame and holding high Carnival on the surface of "The Sun." Inhabitants of "Mercury" were black-skinned women with blonde hair, swathed in brilliantly hued gowns, posing beneath strangely scalloped canopies that seemed to sprout behind their shoulders. Hurling through space on a blazing chunk of metal, the green and yellow riders of "A Comet" clutched fistfuls of lightning bolts, their facial features contorted in a series of deranged grimaces. The residents of "Saturn," six arms extending from their insectlike carapaces, cavorted on sun-drenched plains, beneath enormous golden cacti. Such were the wonders that rolled through the streets of New Orleans and passed into memory with every night parade of the Carnival, a dozen years before the early cinematic marvels of Georges Melies.

There were fewer flights of fancy in the period costuming for the 1888 production, "Legends of the Middle Ages," with its cast of knights, fair maids, squires, soldiers, and attendants. The Bonnecaze plates for "The Hindoo Heavens" (1889) were unlike anything else she ever designed: detailed gouache renderings of authentic Indian costumes painted in the Indian style and palette. Scenes from "Kalevala" (1893) and "Asgard and the Gods" (1895) featured medieval Scandinavian robes and helmets, but among the former were a number of more ethereal costumes for "Snowflakes" and the "Daughters of Fog."

Proteus turned to *The Arabian Nights* in 1891 for "Tales of the Genii," with a host of magicians and enchanters, good and evil genii, and floats depicting "The Altar of Fire," "The Room of Statues," "The Fatal Pavilion," and "The Waters of Oblivion." The most stunning costumes in the pageant were designed for the cast members of "The Evil Genii," with Bonnecaze touches everywhere—in the individual malevolence of their masks, the malignant hues of their body-stocking flesh, and the miniature dragons coiled around their arms and waists. What a strange, frightening vision they must have presented, with their contorted faces leering through the smoking glare of torches.

Proteus led his "A Dream of the Vegetable Kingdom" richly costumed in a gilded tunic, embroidered in brilliants with a large dragonfly, and wearing dragonfly wings. Several floats featured krewe members in a colorful array of winged fairy costumes, and they indeed must have appeared diminutive in this papier-mâché kingdom of enormous lizards and sixteen-feet-high, monumental watermelon. In the most memorable designs, the cast underwent whimsical metamorphoses into plant life, such as sunflowers, corn, thistles, green peas, acorns, and pansies.

The subject for 1894 was the Persian epic, "Shah Nameh," the epic of the kings. Bonnecaze's designs for the large cast of princes, priests, warriors, and kings were rich in Persian motifs, but unlike designs for "The Hindoo Heavens" five years earlier, the plates were not painted in the Mogul manner. Like her costumes for previous historical efforts drawn from the Middle Ages or the exotic East, the Bonnecaze costume plates for "Shah Nameh" were well researched and beautifully painted. They lacked, however, the inspired eccentricity or whimsical invention that infused her finest creations, "Visions of Other Worlds," "A Dream of the Vegetable Kingdom," or above all, her 1896 masterpiece, "Dumb Society."

Carnival pageants and balls of the Golden Age were usually described in newspapers and magazines with breathless superlatives, many of them well deserved, but "masterpiece" was an accolade perhaps too frequently bestowed. The difficulty in attempting description of these fantastic productions was noted long ago by the dean of Carnival historians, Perry Young, who lamented they were "enemies of language that make the loftiest adjectives run pale." So, by the mid-1880s, in their annual process of adjectival exhaustion, newspapers began acclaiming each krewe's parade or ball finer and more brilliant than any previous effort. (This was, of course, artistically impossible and sadly inaccurate, particularly of productions after World War I.) Momus, Proteus, Rex, and Comus were distinct organizations, with distinct personalities and styles; standing within the vast audiences was a smaller band of astute observers and enraptured devotees, those who spent lifetimes appraising these productions.

The Golden Age of Carnival artistry reached its zenith in the closing years of the 1890s, and the season of 1896 was filled with the most scenic brilliance of all. On the stage of the French Opera House, Momus staged the only miniature pageant in Carnival history: eighteen detailed papier-mâché floats illustrating "A Comic History of Rome." Rex presented "Heavenly Bodies," with a remarkable starry invitation and some of Bror Anders Wikstrom's best float designs. Comus, as always, closed Carnival of 1896 with a glittering pageant, "The Months and Seasons of the Year," richly decorated with Jennie Wilde's magical art nouveau flourishes, but the greatest work of this landmark season had rolled the evening before, in the tableaux cars of Proteus, depicting "Dumb Society."

Anthropomorphic images were familiar devices in the masks, costumes, and float designs of Carnival and whimsy was no stranger. What set "Dumb Society" apart, what placed it among Carnival's greatest works was the sly charm and the perfectly pitched humor of Bonnecaze's watercolors. Each of the pageant's eighteen scenes was set amid the papier-mâché decors of nature and featured various members of the animal kingdom, all clothed in human costumes and performing human activities. (Seven of the float plates for this parade may be found in the preceding volume of this series, *Float Designs of the Golden Age.*) Lion presided at the table of "A Royal Banquet," before a group of elegantly clad large cats, a gentle travesty of after-dinner speeches. White mice primped and pranced in organdy pinafores, beneath the steady gazes of "Watchful Guardians," papier-mâché cats standing eighteen feet high.

The Bonnecaze tableaux were neither fables nor satires; there were no morals to be drawn and the occasional barbs (the homely, snooty peahens in "The Upper Crust" and the overdressed monkey in "Five O'Clock Tea") were more like jests, direct but not cutting and tempered with knowing, affectionate, good humor. Indeed, much of the pageant's comedy was to be found in the fanciful costumes and delightful gestures of its cast: the mob-capped Duckling clutching her baby-duck doll, the bespectacled Flamingo fishing in his pink mackintosh; the Rhinoceros and Bison dressed in boxing trunks, and the elegantly liveried and beribboned Ass serving tea. More than a century later, the Bonnecaze paintings for "Dumb Society" remain a wry, one-of-a-kind masterpiece. The cast of this Mardi Gras menagerie appears as lively and winning today as they were on the night they performed their inspired pantomimes.

"Ho-chang."

"Tartar King."

"Dalai Lama."

Carlotta Bonnecaze "Ti Can," water-color costume design for
Proteus pageant, 1885: "Myths and Worships of the Chinese."

"Ti-Hoang."

"Yo."

"Yo."

"Yo."

MESURES

N.° 7.

Jaquette.

1.°	Longueur de taille	48
2.°	Longueur des basques	92
3.°	Carrure	19
4.°	Longueur au coude	52
5.°	Longueur au poignet	84
6.°	Grosseur sous les bras	46
7.°	Grosseur de la taille	41

Pantalon

1.°	Longueur de côté	114
2.°	Longueur d'entre-jambes	83
3.°	Grosseur de ceinture	39

Coiffure

Grosseur de tête	56

Chaussures

En centimètres 27 ½	Points	41

Hauteur totale de la personne 1.ᵐ80

Carlotta Bonnecaze, verso of Proteus costume design,
with measurements of masker.

"Choui."

"Jou."

"Ge."

"Ho."

"Ge."

Carlotta Bonnecaze, "No. 7," water-color costume design for Proteus pageant, 1885: "Myths and Worships of the Chinese."

"Niu-va."

K

"*Assuri.*"

O P

"Gui Hoang."

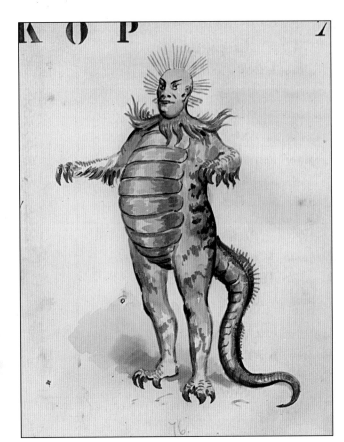

"Gui Hoang."

"Gui Hoang."

Carlotta Bonnecaze, "Fai Hoang," water-color costume design for
Proteus pageant, 1885: "Myths and Worships of the Chinese."

"Kio."

"Ya Yu."

"Pou Ko."

Carlotta Bonnecaze, "Gievah-Hell," water-color float design for Proteus pageant, 1885: "Myths and Worships of the Chinese."

Carlotta Bonnecaze, "Proteus," water-color costume design for Proteus pageant, 1886: "Visions of Other Worlds."

"Salamander."

"Mercurian."

"Salamander."

"Martian Woman."

"Mandolin."

"Accordion."

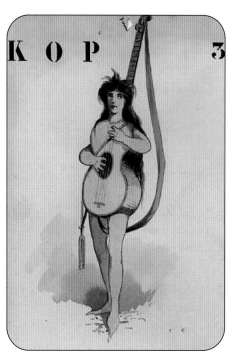

"Guitar."

"Floran."

"Floran."

"Conch."

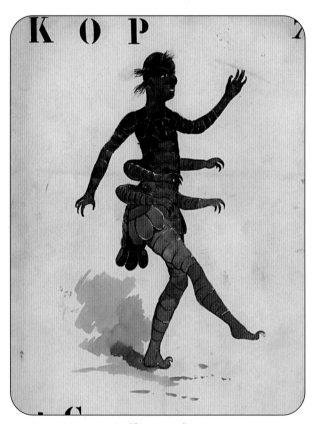

"Saturnian."

"*Cometan.*"

"*Cometan.*"

Carlotta Bonnecaze, "No. 1, Swayambuvha," water-color costume design for Proteus pageant, 1889: "The Hindoo Heavens."

"Fire Spirit."

"Brahma."

"Mohiny."

*"Planet." (Aries) (The float, "Surya, God of the
Sun," appears on page 145 of* Float Designs of
the Golden Age.*)*

"Planet." (Cancer)

"Planet." (Taurus)

"Planet." (Sagittarius)

Sea Nymph

Carlotta Bonnecaze, "Sea Nymph," water-color costume design for Proteus pageant, 1889: "The Hindoo Heavens."

Carlotta Bonnecaze, "Evil Genius," water-color costume
design for Proteus pageant, 1891: "Tales of the Genii."

"Genius."

"Genius."

Carlotta Bonnecaze, "Proteus," water-color costume design for Proteus pageant, 1892: "A Dream of the Vegetable Kingdom."

"Thistle."

"Fungus."

"Fungus."

"Sea Plant."

Carlotta Bonnecaze, "Fern," water-color costume
designs for Proteus pageant, 1892: "A Dream of the
Vegetable Kingdom." (The float appears on page 49 of
Float Designs of the Golden Age.)

Carlotta Bonnecaze, "Slave," water-color costume design for Proteus pageant, 1894: "Shah Nameh."

Carlotta Bonnecaze, "High Priest," water-color costume design for Proteus pageant, 1894: "Shah Nameh."

Carlotta Bonnecaze, "Ass," water-color costume design for Proteus pageant, 1896: "Dumb Society." (The float design, "Five O'Clock Tea," appears on page 51 of Float Designs of the Golden Age.)

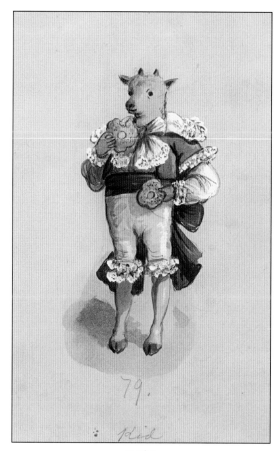

"Kid."

"Sheep."

"Pig."

"Monkey."

Carlotta Bonnecaze, "Lion," water-color costume design for Proteus pageant, 1896: "Dumb Society." (The float design, "A Royal Banquet," appears on page 52 of Float Designs of the Golden Age.)

"Cat."

"Cat."

"Cicada."

"Shrimp."

"Seahorse."

"Hen."

"Heron."

"Vulture."

"Stork."

"Butterfly."

"Duckling."

"Duck."

Carlotta Bonnecaze, "Rooster," water-color costume
design for Proteus pageant, 1896: "Dumb Society."

"Rooster."

Carlotta Bonnecaze, "Mouse," water-color costume designs for Proteus pageant, 1896: Dumb Society. (The float design, "Watchful Guardians," appears on page 52 of Float Designs of the Golden Age.)

"Rat."

"Rat."

Carlotta Bonnecaze, "Frog," water-color costume designs for
Proteus pageant, 1896: Dumb Society. (The float, "At Spanish
Fort," appears on page 53 of Float Designs of the Golden Age.)

"Pelican."

"Flamingo."

"Dragonfly."   *"Butterfly."*

Carlotta Bonnecaze, "Poodle," water-color costume
design for Proteus pageant, 1896: "Dumb Society."

"Peacock."

Carlotta Bonnecaze, "Peacock," water-color costume design for Proteus
pageant, 1896: "Dumb Society." (The float design, "The Upper
Crust," appears on page 50 of Float Designs of the Golden Age.)

CHAPTER III

BROR ANDERS WIKSTROM

ror Anders Wikstrom was one of the most prominent figures in nineteenth-century New Orleans art circles. An acclaimed painter and illustrator, Wikstrom founded the literary journal, *Arts and Letters,* and together with William and Ellsworth Woodward, was a founder of the Art Association of New Orleans. He was also acknowledged as the dean of Carnival artists, and yet given all this, far more of his work disappeared than was saved. He designed the Rex pageants for twenty-five years, from 1885 to 1910, each year creating twenty water-color plates for floats and a hundred or more for costumes. The album of float designs for the 1910 parade, "Freaks of Fable," and a few dozen costume plates are all that survive.

Wikstrom enjoyed some assistance in this work, primarily in the painting of costume plates. When his good friend and colleague, Ellsworth Woodward, created the art department of Newcomb College in 1897, the first students began to work with the noted

Carnival designer, the beginning of an important and enduring relationship.

Beginning around 1897, Wikstrom also designed the Proteus pageants. Two hundred of those glorious water-color float plates, from ten of the thirteen years that he painted for Proteus, have survived, together with six near-complete collections of costume designs. Most of the Carnival artists enjoyed other careers as lithographers, illustrators, or teachers; only Wikstrom was a painter, and his love of painting, his elegant draftsmanship, and his recurring fondness for classical robes, costumes, and decorative motifs distinguish much of his work.

Wikstrom succeeded his fellow Swede and friend Charles Briton as the Rex designer, and he completed the transition to grandeur begun with the 1881 pageant, "Arabian Nights Tales." Costumes for that production were lavishly praised in a souvenir newspaper edition of *New Orleans Carnival*:

"The costumes were of the finest materials; the silks, satins, and laces were of such excellent quality that they would have borne comparison with the costume of the fairest lady in the land. The cars upon which these figures [maskers] were mounted, in carefully studied tableaux and groupings, showed that a master head had planned and an accomplished hand executed their designs. The costumes were fashioned by the Royal Costumers, Chalain and others of Paris, under the supervision of that cultivated and refined officer of his Majesty's household, the Lord High Chamberlain, who selected in person the silks, laces, and other materials, and who gave directions as to the combinations of colors, the shapes and styles of the various articles, and the jewels and trimmings used in their manufacture. The result showed that the master mind that had been at work, for the universal verdict was that in every detail the costumes had reached the pinnacle of perfection."

The Lord High Chamberlain of Rex was the organization's manager, a title later changed to captain. George H. Braughn, Rex's third manager, served from 1876 through 1889. He worked year round in absolute secrecy, and when he led the Rex procession on horseback Mardi Gras mornings, he was fully masked. Braughn was the discerning gentleman who journeyed to Paris every year of his term to choose fabrics, trimmings, and jewels, carrying with him designs by artists whose identities also remained guarded secrets. When the great Charles Briton died in 1884, his brief obituary made no mention of his Carnival work.

The beginning of Wikstrom's Mardi Gras career magically coincided with the advent of color lithography. From 1885 through 1909, all of Wikstrom's lost float plates were fortunately reproduced as vivid chromolithographs in the Rex Carnival editions. Miniature reproductions of the floats in these parade papers were remarkably faithful to most details in the original designs, including many of the costumes. By comparing Wikstrom's costume plates to floats in the Carnival Bulletins, we have been able to identify several as Rex designs: red-gowned Charity from "Symbolism of Colors" (1892); white-robed Pleiad from "Heavenly Bodies" (1896); and two ladies bountiful, Peas and Strawberries, from "Harvest Queens" (1898).

Wikstrom frequently turned to realms of fancy for Rex. "Visions" (1891) included characters from "Fairy Land," "Demonia," and "Folly." Angels and elves abounded in the papier-mâché "Fantasies" of 1893—in "Star Land," "Fairies' Court," "Silver Sprays," and "Dream Land." Among the "Chronicles of Fairy Land," Rex's subject for 1895, were "Moon Fairies Before Oberon," "Revelries of Titania's Court," and "At the Shrine of Celestial Light." "Reveries of Rex" (1899) daydreamed of "Crystal Caves," "Forest of Enchantment," "Isle of Delight," and "Pavilion of the Gods."

It was not uncommon in Golden Age pageants for half the krewe members to cross-dress: males costumed as storybook princesses; winged, star-veiled fairies; or women of the ancient world, complete with gowns, wigs, and lovely masks. Females appeared in even greater numbers in many Wikstrom tableaux, and almost exclusively in two of his fancies, "Harvest Queens" (1898) and "Idealistic Queens" (1905), which included the Queens of Brightness, Fashion, Gaiety, Love, Mystery, The Beautiful, and Strife.

The six existing collections of Wikstrom's costume designs for Proteus begin with "A Trip to Wonderland," the 1898 papier-mâché tour of "A New Heaven," "The Sparkling Vineyard," "The Devil's Basket," "Love's Hammock," and "Down the Rapids." Along the way, in these beautifully painted water-color plates, we encounter a host of devils, human flowers, and fairies clad in velvet breeches, petaled capes, and satin robes. The "Wonderland" designs conclude with a delightful surprise, the earliest extant costume plates for a captain and his aides. Captain, not king, was the true ruler in the fantastic empire of Carnival. Mysterious captains, masked, plumed, and accompanied by their mounted aides, appeared at the head of every procession; the masked gods and bearded kings who followed on their respective floats were potent symbols and glittering figureheads, their roles enacted every year by another krewe member.

Proteus, swept up in the patriotic fervor of the Spanish-American War, chose "E Pluribus Unum" for his subject in 1899. New Orleans had been deeply moved a year earlier by the destruction of the battleship *Maine* in Havana, the attack that began the war. When the *Maine* arrived for the final week of Carnival in 1897, she was the first battleship ever received in the harbor of New Orleans. Her crew was at liberty to participate in the festivities, and her officers were present at every ball. The first state to be saluted in "E Pluribus Unum" was Maine, with a compliment to the ill-fated vessel.

The pageant, too, proved star-crossed. Facing record cold temperatures and streets strangely covered with ice and snow, Proteus canceled his appearance the night before Mardi Gras. For the first and only time in Carnival history, two evenings after Ash Wednesday, a krewe paraded during lent. It was not a success, and the lack of Carnival spirit was not the only problem. Wikstrom's float and costume designs for "E Pluribus Unum" were the least engaging of his career, as straightforward and familiar as a roll call. Several of the sailor suits and liberty costumes offered amusing variations of Columbia (a popular allegorical figure in the era's graphics), and one float was a wicked delight. "Massachusetts," presented a flinty tableau worthy of Bonnecaze, with its large papier-mâché Plymouth Rock, and its contingent of proper blue-stocking Bostonians—bald and bespectacled eggheaded gentlemen and dour spinsters, one of them clutching an oversized volume of Emerson.

By 1900 Wikstrom had lived in New Orleans for twenty years and was at the peak of his power. And while a Scandinavian chill still hovers over many of his atmospheric marine paintings, his Carnival work reflected an aesthetic acclimation—a seductive, lyrical synthesis of cool, formal neoclassicism and exuberant, tropical abundance.

Wikstrom's fondness for Middle Eastern fantasies reasserts itself in the last three collections of his costume plates: "Al Kyris the Magnificent" (1901), "Cleopatra" (1903), and "The Rubaiyat" (1905). In these designs, the high priests and priestesses, wizards, warriors, musicians, poets, and fates are all swathed in flowing satin robes and gowns, diaphanous veils and velvet capes, bejeweled vests, and sequined sashes.

"The Rubaiyat" costume plates offer an additional and historic bonanza, the only surviving set of designs for the cast's paraphernalia. Dozens of watercolor renderings depict a profusion of masks, wigs, beards, and moustaches; myriad slippers, sandals, and leggings; as well as an assortment of necklaces and bracelets. Moreover, there are drawings for the numerous stage properties held by the maskers—the wands, horns, lyres, swords, staffs, fans, and chalices. In Wikstrom's sumptuous water-color float designs, we revel in his artistry; in his hastily painted inventory of theatrical paraphernalia, we are left to marvel at the breadth of vision and amazing attention to detail of these Golden Age tableaux.

__	Anklet
⊠	Armlet *ac illuos*
⊠	Belt X
⊠	Bracelets X
__	Cloak
__	Coat
__	Dagger
⊠	Drapery X
⊠	Dress
⊠	Gloves *422*
__	Hat
__	Hauberk
⊠	Headdress
⊠	Hood *422*
__	Necklace
⊠	Property X2
__	Sash
⊠	Shirt *422*
⊠	Shoes
__	Skirt
__	Stockings
__	Sword
⊠	Tights *422*
__	Trousers
⊠	Trunks
__	Tunic
⊠	Wig
__	Wings

Bror Anders Wikstrom, "Jupiter Tonans," water-color costume design for unknown pageant, circa 1895.

Bror Anders Wikstrom, "Plenty," water-color costume design for Proteus pageant, 1899: "E Pluribus Unum."

"Liberty."

"Army."

"Navy."

"Bostonian."

"Bostonian."

"Bostonian."

"Sugar."

"Cotton."

"Rice."

"Louisiana."

Bror Anders Wikstrom, "No. 1, Proteus,"
watercolor costume design for Proteus pageant
of 1900, "Tales of Childhood."

13

Princess, "Tales of Childhood."

Bror Anders Wikstrom, "No. 56," costume design for Proteus pageant, 1900: "Tales of Childhood."

"No. 11."

"No. 67."

"Imp."

"Imp."

"Imp."

"Imp."

2 *Goblin*

4 *Goblin*

"*Goblin.*"

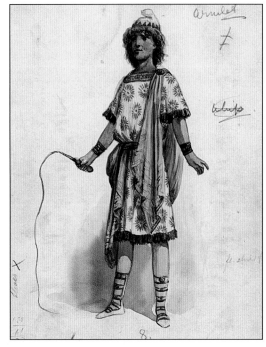

"Night." *"Charioteer."*

*(Float designs for the costumes above, "The Awakening,"
appears on page 70 of* Float Designs of the Golden Age.*)*

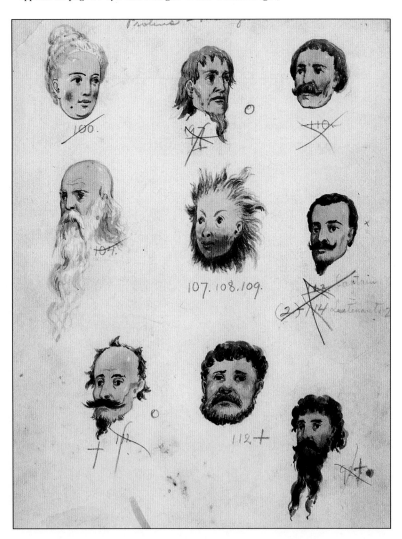

*Bror Anders Wikstrom, "Masks,"
water-color costume design for
Proteus pageant, 1905: "The
Rubaiyat."*

"No. 12."

"No. 62."

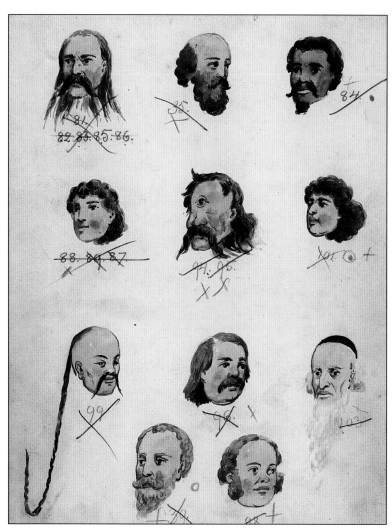

"Masks."

"No. 84."

"No. 83."

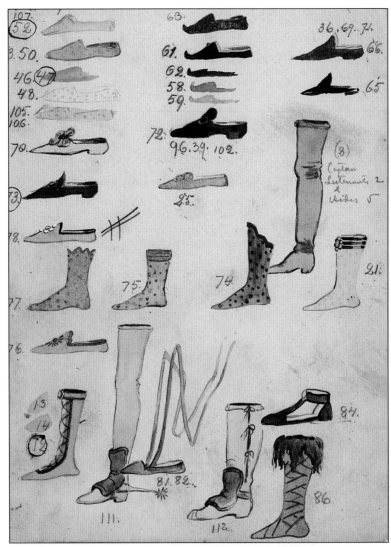

"Footwear."

"No. 28."

"No. 27."

"Assorted Properties."

"Assorted Properties."

"Assorted Properties."

Bror Anders Wikstrom, "No. 18," water-color costume design for Proteus pageant, 1907: "The Queen of the Serpents."

Bror Anders Wikstrom, "The Sea Beasts," water-color float design for Proteus pageant, 1907: "The Queen of the Serpents."

Bror Anders Wikstrom, "Chinese Mythology," water-color float plate for the Proteus silver anniversary pageant, 1906: "The Inspirations of Proteus."

Above: Bror Anders Wikstrom, "Adventures," water-color float design for the Proteus pageant, 1906: "The Inspirations of Proteus."

Opposite, top: Bror Anders Wikstrom, "The Castle of Jewels," water-color float design for Proteus pageant, 1907: "The Queen of the Serpents."

Opposite, bottom: Bror Anders Wikstrom, "The Tomb of Solomon," water-color float design for the Proteus pageant, 1907: "The Queen of the Serpents."

*Bror Anders Wikstrom, "The Heavens," water-color float design for
the Proteus pageant, 1906: "The Inspirations of Proteus."*

CHAPTER IV

JENNIE WILDE

The Mardi Gras-night parades of Comus were already an institution when Jennie Wilde began to design them. From the early 1870s until his death in 1884, Charles Briton designed the floats and costumes for the Mistick Krewe. From the years 1885 to 1889, Comus staged neither parade nor ball, and when he returned in 1890, he found the night contested—the Krewe of Proteus had adopted the revered Tuesday evening and refused to give it up. For the first and only time in Carnival history, two rival pageants—Proteus's "Elfland" and Comus's "Palingenesis"—collided on Canal Street. Comus won the right of way; Proteus paraded once more on Tuesday, without incident, and then returned to his traditional Monday night. The 1890 "Palingenesis of the Mistick Krewe" was the only Comus parade designed by Wikstrom. In the following Carnival season, Jennie Wilde, then twenty-five, made her debut with a dramatic flourish—invitations to the Comus ball depicted a large green, armor-plated serpent, coiled and striking upon a card of bronze.

Thus began one of Carnival's most fabled collaborations, winning new accolades for Comus and ongoing acclaim for the young artist. Wilde came from a distinguished Irish Catholic family of jurists, writers, and poets, and in an era when professional opportunities for women were rare, she enjoyed success as an artist, designer, and poet. Her poetry appeared regularly in New Orleans newspapers and in literary journals, to which she also contributed numerous illustrations.

The only surviving paintings by Jennie Wilde are her ink and water-color plates for Comus pageants and balls. In these inspired fantasias for floats and costumes (augmented by chromolithographed parade papers), we follow Wilde's artistic evolution, from the primitively painted forests and glens of "Demonology" (1891) to the fiery clouds and showers of gilded crescents in "Flights of Fancy" (1909) or "Tales from Chaucer" (1914). Her earliest costume plates, from "Nippon, the Land of the Rising Sun" (1892), offered Carnivalesque re-creations of authentic Japanese robes and uniforms; like her float plates from this period, several of them were dusted with glitter.

Miss Winnie Davis, daughter of former Confederate president Jefferson Davis, reigned as Comus's queen over the "Nippon" production, designed in its entirety by Jennie Wilde. This was the only Comus ball at which the queen and court were attired in thematic costumes, Miss Davis in a magnificent ecru silk-satin kimono, embroidered with large golden chrysanthemums and sunrays of colored stones.

The queen's scepter had a paste cabochon ruby as the sun's center, surrounded by radiating filaments of gold, the highest of which was tipped with dewdrop pearls of gold, and all supported a lifelike golden spider and web. The golden cup carried by Comus, encrusted with red, green, and yellow stones, was presented after the ball to his queen. Cup and scepter, along with other jewels worn that evening, remain on display at the Confederate Museum in New Orleans, beneath an oil portrait of Miss Davis in her royal robes. Enshrined across the room is one of the Civil War's most curious relics: a crown of thorns made by the hands of Pope Pius IX and sent in sympathy to Jefferson Davis.

Jennie Wilde was reared in the triumphant Catholicism of Vatican I and the pontificate of Pius IX—when the church's sacred rituals were celebrated in Latin, with bejeweled vestments, clouds of incense, and glorious theatricality. Wilde, who painted the interior murals of the Church of Notre Dame de Bon Secours on Jackson Avenue, was steeped in this ecclesiastical magnificence. She was also fascinated throughout her career with the painting and literature of the symbolists and the decadents, with the chimeras and operatic grandeur of Gustave Moreau and Gustave Flaubert, the sensually tinted worlds of Pierre Loti, and the Babylonian apocalypses of Jean Rochegrosse. Nurtured on this other-worldly splendor, Wilde in turn called forth visions of exotic temples and molten clouds, bowers of gigantic flora, and enchanted beasts.

Wilde became Carnival's high priestess of art nouveau, and the float plates of her maturity were animated by her hallmark dynamic energy—by turns elegant, frenzied, and spellbinding. The figures in Wilde's costume designs were less lively, sometimes clumsily drawn, and while her whimsical costumes possessed a naïve charm, they invited no comparison to the mastery of Carlotta Bonnecaze. In the costumes for three pageants from Wilde's late period—those for "Gods and Goddesses" (1908), "Flights of Fancy" (1909), "Mahomet" (1910), and "Tales from Chaucer" (1914)—we are left to revel in some of Carnival's most lavish relics. The robes, tunics, and flowing mantels in these designs were ablaze with gold, and many of the maskers wore crowns, princely turbans, or bejeweled helmets. In their outstretched hands, the cast held a dazzling assortment of precious objects—golden staffs and scepters, incense burners, strands of bells, and wands tipped with cryptic symbols.

Among the many illusions made real in the pageants and balls of Carnival, perhaps the most prevalent was that of fantastic, inconceivable wealth. Year after year the glimmering Mardi Gras tableaux presented visions of boundless riches, embellished with an insistent histrionic extravagance so complete that even scenes from nature were dappled with gold and silver leaf. Comus not only introduced this aesthetic of opulence, but had also come to embody it. The grandest, most bewitching flourishes of that aesthetic began in 1900, with Wilde's designs for "Stories of the Golden Age," and continued for more than a decade with her final work, "Tales from Chaucer," in 1914, a triumphant collaboration with artist and krewe at the peaks of their powers.

In the long line of designers for Comus, no one contributed more to his brilliance than Jennie Wilde, and in the august line of Comus captains, none served a longer term than S. P. Walmsley, the ruling personality in Carnival for a quarter century. The grandest years of their twenty-five-year tenures overlapped, creating a unique Carnival relationship. At the Comus Ball of 1892, Wilde was the recipient of a special honor, as reported by the *Picayune*: "The Captain [Walmsley's predecessor] presented her with a jeweled necklace and his cloak, a rich affair of blue silk velvet shot with pearls and embroidered with gold."

Walmsley was captain when the Mistick Krewe celebrated its golden anniversary in 1906 (the first such occasion in the history of Carnival) with the pageant "The Masque of Comus." At the ball that followed, the krewe again honored Wilde, presenting her with a large crystal replica of the cup carried by Comus, with "Comus" and the date wrought in silver. Two years later, when the captain's lovely daughter, Myra, reigned as Queen of Comus, the fabled debutante reviewed the procession, "Gods and Goddesses," from the balcony of the Pickwick Club. Miss Walmsley then proceeded in her carriage to the ball at the French Opera House, where every detail of throne setting or costume was designed by Wilde.

"Time's Mysteries" (1913) was the last Comus production Jennie Wilde lived to see. The following summer, on vacation in England, Wilde became ill and sought to convalesce in a Measden convent, where she died on September 11. She lay at rest in Metairie Cemetery on Mardi Gras night 1914, when Comus appeared with "Tales from Chaucer," but her drawings for that parade and several others were soon resurrected. The Comus pageants of 1915, "Lore and Legends of Childhood," and 1916, "Glimpses of the World of Modern Art," were designed by Blanche Preston Preston. The lithographed Carnival Bulletins featuring the Preston floats are so laden with Wilde motifs they are readily mistaken for the work of the latter—not so con-

cerning the surviving handful of Preston's watercolor plates, which seem pale and lifeless. Following this two-year interregnum, Preston, a native of West Virginia, returned home, and Comus returned to his collected works of Jennie Wilde.

The Comus production of 1917, "Romantic Legends," presented floats that were stunning re-creations chosen from Wilde's most beautiful designs. Comus was enthroned beneath a golden crown and flowing canopy of cloth of gold, papier-mâché extravagance, lifted from the same molds created years earlier in 1911, when Comus presented "Familiar Quotations." Also reappearing from 1911 was Cleopatra's burnished vessel, "The Barge She Sat In," which in 1917 became "The Lady of the Nile." "Romantic Legends" was the last Mardi Gras before the onset of World War I and also marked the last appearance of Comus for seven years.

When Comus returned in 1924 with "The Mirthful Monarch Greets Ye Once Again," S. P. Walmsley was still captain, and Wilde's remarkable posthumous career was briefly resumed. Twelve years after "Time's Mysteries" and her death, Wilde's fabulous swan song came with the Comus parade of 1925, "The Realms of Phantasy," a re-creation of her marvelous designs for 1909's "Flights of Fancy." Few people saw "Flights of Fancy," which had left the den in threatening weather and was quickly engulfed in a raging thunderstorm. Fewer still among the teeming throngs lining the parade route in 1925 suspected, or were ever meant to know of, the magnificent history unfolding that Mardi Gras night.

Jennie Wilde, "No. 15," water-color costume design for Comus pageant, 1892: "Nippon, Land of the Rising Sun."

Jennie Wilde, "No. 32," water-color design for Comus
pageant, 1892: "Nippon, Land of the Rising Sun."

Jennie Wilde, "No. 104," water-color costume design on vellum for Comus pageant, 1908: "Gods and Goddesses."

Jennie Wilde, "No. 107," water-color costume design on vellum for Comus pageant, 1908: "Gods and Goddesses." (The notation "1925" in pencil confirms that Wilde's costume and float designs from 1908 were resurrected for the 1925 pageant.)

Jennie Wilde, "Comus," water-color costume design for Comus pageant, 1909. (Wilde incorporated pansies into every aspect of the 1909 productions. Comus led the pageant, "Flights of Fancy," enthroned in a bower of papier-mâché pansies, his costume and his queen's costume were ablaze with jeweled pansies, and the dance card for the ball was a large die-cut pansy. The float design, "Comus, No. 1 Car," appears on page 97 of Float Designs of the Golden Age.)

Jennie Wilde ········ 101 ········

Jennie Wilde, "No. 34," water-color costume design
for Comus pageant, 1909: "Flights of Fancy."

"No. 123."

"No. 100."

*Jennie Wilde, "No. 9," water-color costume design
on vellum for Comus pageant, 1910: "Mahomet."*

"No. 8."

"No. 10."

"No. 17."

"No. 20."

"No. 16."

Jennie Wilde, "Legend of Eyla," water-color float design for Comus pageant,
1910: "Mahomet." (The costumes on the opposite page appear on this float.)

"No. 13."

Jennie Wilde, "No. 12," water-color costume design for Comus pageant, 1910: "Mahomet."

"No. 15."

"No. 22."

*Jennie Wilde, "No. 40," water-color costume design on
vellum for Comus pageant, 1910: "Mahomet."*

"No. 98."

"No. 84."

"No. 108."

"No. 109."

110

XXXX

"No. 110."

Jennie Wilde, "No. 32," water-color costume design on vellum for Comus pageant, 1914: "Tales from Chaucer."

"No. 20."

Jennie Wilde, "No. 31," water-color costume design for
Comus pageant, 1914: "Tales from Chaucer."

1914

Jennie Wilde, water-color costume design on vellum for Comus pageant, 1914: "Tales from Chaucer." (The float design, "St. Cecilia," appears of page 109 of Float Designs of the Golden Age.)

"Saint Cecilia."

"No. 94."

"No. 93."

Jennie Wilde, "No. 106," water-color costume design on vellum for Comus pageant, 1914: "Tales from Chaucer." (Float design appears on page 110 of Float Designs of the Golden Age.*)*

Jennie Wilde, "Captain," water-color costume design on vellum for captain of Comus pageant, 1908. (S. P. Walmsley was captain of the Mistick Krewe in 1908, and his daughter,
Myra, reigned that year as Queen of Comus. When Comus returned after a seven-year
hiatus in 1924, Walmsley still served as captain, and the decision to resurrect Wilde's
designs could only have been his. In 1925, the float and costume designs from the 1908

CHAPTER V

CENEILLA ALEXANDER AND LOUIS FISCHER

The early lives of Ceneilla Bower and Jennie Wilde contain a number of striking parallels. Between 1864 and 1865 both women were born into families of prominent jurists in Georgia: Bower in Bainbridge, Wilde in Augusta. They both went on to study art in New York, then moved on to New Orleans, where each became a celebrated Carnival designer. Wilde's move to New Orleans was actually a return, for her family was already well established in the city's legal, literary, and social circles. Ceneilla Bower came to the city a few years after her marriage to the Rev. William McFadden Alexander, a Presbyterian clergyman. After serving as pastor in Bainbridge, then Memphis, Tennessee, the Reverend Alexander came to New Orleans, where for forty-one years he served as pastor of the Prytania Street Presbyterian Church. Ceneilla Bower Alexander established herself as a dutiful wife and mother, as well as one of Carnival's finest artists; throughout both careers she was known as Mrs. Alexander.

A meager handful of Alexander's early work has survived, the earliest being three costume designs for the Krewe of Nereus in 1897. To these lovely pen-and-ink drawings of Nereus, Nereid, and Flying Fish, Alexander applied delicate washes of pale sea green or pink, dotted with tiny beads of white and folds of silver. This judicious use of color, which remained one of Alexander's hallmarks, might have been gleaned from Sir Francis Bacon's essay, "On Masques and Triumphs": "The colours that shew best by candle-light are white, carnation, and a kind of sea-water-green, and oes and spangs [small metallic discs sewn on to reflect light] as they are of no great cost, so they are of the most glory." Following the Nereus designs, the next record of Alexander's work came in 1911, when she succeeded Wikstrom as the designer of Rex.

Alexander's float designs, like Jennie Wilde's, celebrated the extravagance and carefree excess of Carnival's over-the-top aesthetic—but in a totally different style. Wilde's visions of flaming clouds, golden crescents, and gilded bowers rolled in the great night parades of Comus, in the magical light of torches and smoking, sparkling flares. Alexander's creations rolled in the daylight processions of Rex, in the brilliant morning and midday winter suns of New Orleans. Wilde's visions were aglow with sorcery and spectral power, Alexander's radiated exquisite abundance and Belle Epoque grandeur. Alexander was a superb draftsman, the finest since Charles Briton, and her lavish drawings for Rex were alive not only with technical virtuosity, but also with the great pleasure one senses she derived in creating them.

This love of drawing also infused Alexander's costume plates. Having once finished a costume design, she was occasionally compelled to add yet another element, like the large open book lying behind her "Flying Fish," or to sketch a second view of a headpiece or prop to be carried by the masker. Alexander frequently drew the cast members in profile, and many of those plates were embellished with her delightful thumbnail sketches.

The versos of the costume plates, like her preliminary float designs, were filled with copious notes of explanation and direction. Alexander's float notations often became choruses of exasperation; she had little regard for Georges Soulie, the master float builder, or his successor, and less for his partner, Henry Crassons, an accomplished scenic painter. "That horrible Rex car! Whole back left off! If Mr. Soulie, when he first looks at the sketches would tell us what he can't make, or WON'T make, right THEN I could change to something he COULD make instead of crippling the float by leaving a perfect blank where some frequently important art object was." Alexander's costume notations were more civil, explaining her choice of fabrics, followed by explicit instructions regarding trim, beading, or brilliants. Yet even those directions tended toward harangues, with Alexander's feverish penmanship growing desperately ever smaller as it neared the bottom of the page; unstoppable, and indecipherably, she struggled on to the paper's edges and corners.

Among the Carnival artists, Mrs. Alexander was the lone diva, and her difficulty in working with others may have contributed to her early retire-ment. The Rex parade of 1923, "A Fantasy of the Sea," was her last, although she continued for several years to design costumes for the king himself. Sometime during 1923, Alexander learned of the Comus plans to return the following year, and submitted a design for the throne set to the captain, S. P. Walmsley. In October, the captain's daughter, Myra, tactfully responded to Alexander: "The beautiful designs arrived safely, also your two letters which were very explicit and easily understood in every way. . . . The only trouble being the fear that they cannot afford this year to build such an expensive throne. . . . They are delighted with it. . . . It is a lovely PICTURE, too pretty not to last forever."

While Alexander designed Rex, she had occasional assistance with the costume plates from students at Newcomb College, an arrangement that began with the friendship of Wikstrom and Ellsworth Woodward. Among the students Woodward guided toward the arcane world of Carnival design was a precocious young woman, Louis Andrews. Miss Andrews was sixteen years old when she entered Newcomb in 1917; two years later, she designed several of the costumes for the Rex pageant, "Life's Pilgrimage," and continued to work with Alexander, and with Anne McKinne Robertson, an artist whose Carnival career remains largely undocumented. A flamboyant presence at Newcomb, Andrews was admired as an artist but renowned for her wit. She was usually attired in tweed jackets and neckties but also made dramatic appearances on campus in the costumes of various nationalities. Shortly before her graduation in 1921, Andrews was the likely author as well as the designer of the booklet for the Knights of Momus Ball, *The Battle of Don Carnival with Lady Lent*.

A resident of the Pontalba apartments for most of her life, Louis Andrews was at the epicenter of the literary and artistic bohemia that flourished in New Orleans during the 1920s. Artists and writers were drawn to the picturesque French Quarter, with its fabulous textures, tropical manners, and inexpensive rents. Sherwood Anderson, the Pulitzer Prize-winning novelist, was a leading light. In 1921 two young natives, Albert Goldstein and

Julius Friend, cofounded *The Double Dealer,* in which they published works by then unknown Hart Crane, William Faulkner, and Edmund Wilson. Faulkner wrote his first novel in an apartment overlooking the garden behind the Saint Louis Cathedral, and he also wrote the introduction to *Sherwood Anderson and Other Famous Creoles,* a small book by William Spratling of forty drawings of artists, writers, and personalities of the Vieux Carré. Andrews created the book's thoughtful pen-and-ink portrait of Spratling, infusing it with admiration and affection. In Spratling's caricature of her, Andrews appeared clutching a handful of brushes and pens, with her smartly bobbed hair and the huge, unfortunate nose that was her curse.

Following her marriage to Lawrence Fischer in 1926, they continued to live in the Pontalba, where for decades they hosted frequent gatherings and encouraged fledgling members of the artistic, literary, and theatrical worlds. The fabulous Carnival career of Louis Andrews Fischer was in full swing throughout the 1920s. By the time of her marriage, Fischer had designed parades and costumes for Rex, Momus, and Proteus, as well as invitations for Comus and The Mystic Club. She had also begun her lifelong work as chief scenic designer for W. H. B. Spangenberg, the company that produced almost all of the Carnival balls.

It is our misfortune that little of Fischer's early work has survived. Her designs for the 1922 Proteus pageant, "Romance of the Rose," are the only set of float plates. A handful of her 1923 designs for "Alice in Wonderland" are the sole remnants of Momus, and a few costume designs and a small sketchbook of preliminary float drawings for "The Jewels of Rex" (1930) are all that remains of her work for Rex. Like her mentor, Mrs. Alexander, Fischer was a superb draftsman. She also happened to be the first Carnival designer born in the twentieth century, and high among the eclectic influences in her work was her passion for the brilliant sets and costumes of the

Ballets Russes. Fischer's costumes for Pearl and Moonstone, delicately shaded layers of chiffon, recalled the flowing robes and gowns of Alexander's muselike Oracle, and the lithe female figures in their lyrical drawings were all dancing. But while any number of Alexander or Fischer's costumes would have been at home on the stages of Paris or Monte Carlo, the delicate raiment they designed was draped upon the stolid frames of prominent New Orleans businessmen who, in Mardi Gras enchantments, became dancers for a day.

The unlikely perfection of those transformations provoked choruses of explication and exasperation from Alexander. Fischer, on the other hand, relished the genial mischief and occasionally sublime comedy of such moments, and she continued to populate Rex pageants with a host of women— Southern belles in hoop skirts, pioneer women in gingham and bonnets, queens Elizabeth, Antoinette, and Victoria. The Rex subject in 1924 depicted "Notable Women Adown the Ages," among them Salome, Jezebel, Joan of Arc, and Lucrezia Borgia. For his 1925 pageant, Rex presented "Romances of Fan Land," with tableaux of "The Egyptian Flabellum," "The Poisoned Fan of the Medicis," and "The Fans of Watteau."

Fischer's lavish designs for "The Jewels of Rex" were completed before the onset of the Great Depression in 1930. The immediate effects of the Depression could be seen in the cutbacks and economies of the Rex parade of 1931 "The Story of the Drama." The first Carnival pageant to survey the theater, this was also Fischer's final parade for Rex. Among the eighteen delightful scenes were "The Greek Drama," "The Roman Spectacle," "The Comedia dell'Arte," "Miracle and Morality Plays," "Shakespeare's Plays," "Restoration Comedy," "The Circus," and "Show Boat." In Fischer's theatrical farewell to float designing, a departure lasting more than thirty years, Float No. 17 was, of course, "The Russian Ballet."

*Ceneilla Bower Alexander, "King Nereus," water-color costume design
for Krewe of Nereus Ball, 1897: "Coral Groves and Grottoes."*

Ceneilla Bower Alexander, "Flying Fish," water-color costume design for Krewe of Nereus Ball, 1897: "Coral Groves and Grottoes."

Ceneilla Bower Alexander, "Nereid," water-color costume design for Krewe of Nereus Ball, 1897: "Coral Groves and Grottoes."

Ceneilla Bower Alexander, "Painting," water-color costume design for Rex pageant, 1911: "Arts and Sciences."

"Horticulture."

"Horticulture."

Ceneilla Bower Alexander, "Childhood," water-color costume design for Rex pageant, 1920: "Life's Pilgrimage."

Ceneilla Bower Alexander, "Page," water-color costume design for Rex pageant, circa 1920.

"Pan."

"Unholy Love."

Ceneilla Bower Alexander, "Success in Love," water-color costume design for Rex pageant, 1920: "Life's Pilgrimage." (This design appears to have been worked on by an assistant. Alexander notes several corrections and writes of the "joy bells": "If they actually tinkle 'twill be all the better.")

"Goddess of Fortune."

"Youth Inquiring at the Oracle."

Ceneilla Bower Alexander, "Angel in Armor," water-color costume design for Rex pageant, 1920: "Life's Pilgrimage."

Ceneilla Bower Alexander, "Good and Evil Cast Lots for the Soul," water-color costume design for Rex pageant, 1920: "Life's Pilgrimage."

(CBA)

Explanation of Drapery.

The drapery used here is made of one long width of material several yds long, and of a good width, depending on the height of the wearer.

Use plenty of silver in this costume as well as the gold (float has much silver) as in borders etc. Wreath solid silver, also stars. (palms)

Fig 1   Fig 2   Fig 3

Gold Scale-armor

upper Selvedge   upper Selvedge   upper Selvedge

C   L   L   L.E.

L.E.   P   K   L.E.

Slash the material here crosswise to a sufficient depth & drawn it across to cover the back and fasten at left shoulder. L.S. Fig 4

"Tabs of cloth-of-gold" bound or edged with silver

Fig 4

The piece of material is caught in one hand at the corner (See C, Fig 1) and the edge or selvedge is caught in the other hand somewhat like a loop (L, Fig 1) and the two are tied into an ordinary, simple Knot, K, Fig 3 (Also see K on costume plate). An ornamental pin, P Fig 3, is then put in a little way from the knot to cause the gap or open in to be a little wider so as to show a little more of the armored costume underneath. The long, free end of the material is then turned backward (See L.E Fig 2 & Fig 3) and brought around the back, upward and caught on the right shoulder in folds, (the upper selvedge still remaining the upper). The long end, after being laid in folds and passing over the shoulder falls (about to the knee) in front in a cascade effect. The lower selvedge (when the material was laid in folds on the right shoulder) fell to a little below the elbow as shown by the dotted red line Fig 4. Here a few inches of the material are cut away to form a wide short "Kimona sleeve. Or, if the material need more fullness the blue line can be folds at the shoulder, with very little cut out for the "Kimona sleeve", and a separate piece = "pieced on" to bring the sleeve to the proper length below the elbow (approximately about "three-quarter" length) Of course after being draped this way, the drapery should be firmly served to the under-costume where necessary and snaps and hooks and eyes put on to fasten it, so the wearer can put it on without any trouble and without having to adjust a single thing himself.

Sword of gold & Selvge & rhinestones. Band across chest of gold & little Rhinestone banding.

L.S.   upper Selvedge   cut edge   slits for wings   cascade end.

Under-tunic of all-over-beaded material (crystal or silver beads) Inset at neck (g, Fig 1) of same, edged with row of Rhinestones.

Ceneilla Bower Alexander, *verso of "Angel in Armor," explanation of drapery, notes in ink.*

(Detail of Wing) "Fig 1"

This costume should not be made of a ~~dead~~ harsh "dead-white", the kind that look chalky, but of a soft ivory white, almost an "oyster-white." The character an "unfettered spirit" ascending; and the lower part of costume is shaded down to the deep coloring shown in plate. If the shaded material can not be found, a good dyer can easily accomplish the shading. The shading is a very important part of the design as it brings the white costume gradually down to the color of the "ground" from which the "spirit" is rising (the float on which the figure stands. There is a special reason for this in the float design. The lower end of the scarf-drapery also is shaded, as it falls below the line where the shading begins.

This costume should be a glittering mass of crystal beads, Rhinestones and pearls as having so little color, it will take all the sparkle you can put into it to make it sufficiently rich.

There is a closely fitted foundation of net over the flesh colored tights,—this net being thickly sprinkled with crystal beads where it shows. (This "all-over" beaded net can be bought ready to use).

Two rows of very deep crystal bead fringe are used on the bodice, and two below the waist line, and one very deep on skirt. Delicate decorations of silver also are used among the "embroideries etc.

The beaded net is also used on the part of skirt that shows through the slash at knee.

→ Omit the net above on right arm.

First row of fring

Second row of fringe—

Fig 2

Main wire

Framework of wing

Crystal bead fringe to be used. not tinsel.

Front without Girdle or Fringe

Fig 3
Wire for one point before it is put on the main wire and before star is added at the end, S.

Wire

Small wires

Wires

S

D

Tulle stretched over the wing frame helps to steady the points or star-supported. the tulle is then cut out at the edge

Crystal beads

Everything but the scarf-drapery is to be made of transparent material — except of course the parts that are made of the beaded

Ceneilla Bower Alexander, verso of "The Unfettered Soul,"
costume details and explanations in ink.

Ceneilla Bower Alexander, "The Unfettered Soul," water-color
costume design for Rex pageant, 1920: "Life's Pilgrimage."

"Hours."

"Galatea."

Ceneilla Bower Alexander, "Death," water-color costume design for unknown pageant, circa 1926.

*Ceneilla Bower Alexander, water-color costume
for Rex, King of Carnival, circa 1920.*

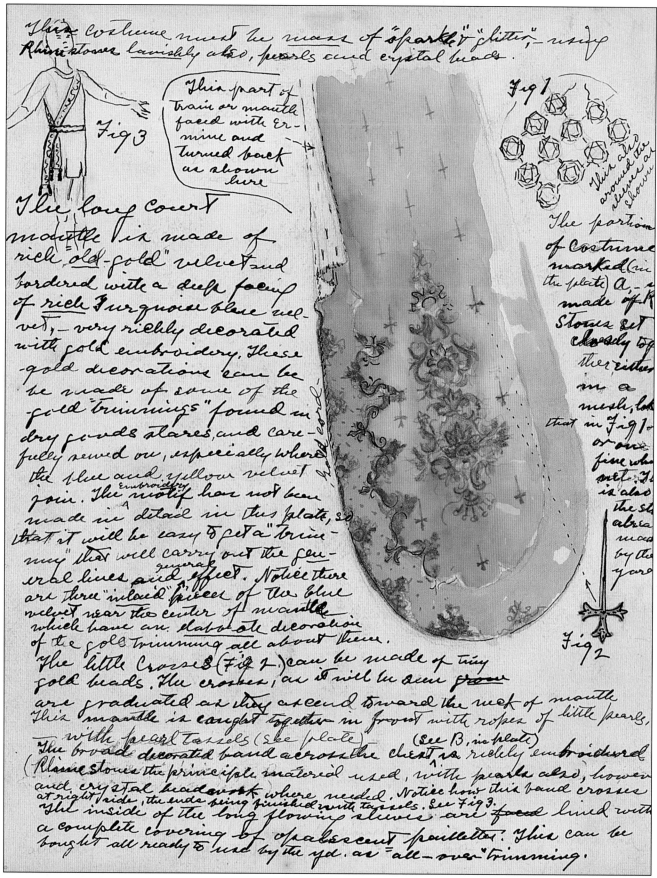

Water-color details and ink notations on verso Rex costume design, circa 1920.

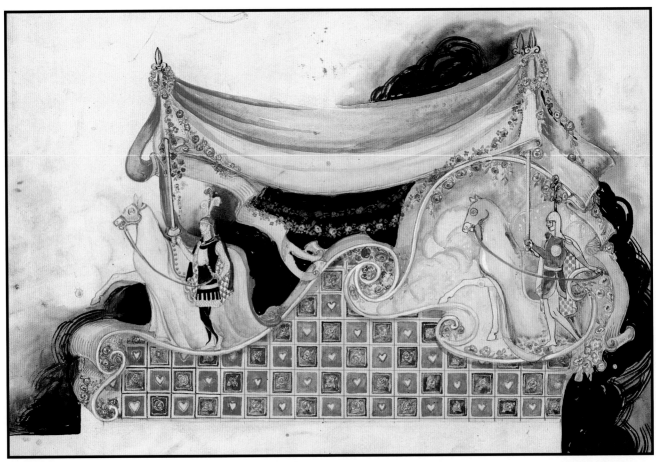

Above: *Louis Andrews Fischer, "The Painted Wall," water-color float design for Proteus pageant, 1922: "Romance of the Rose."*

Opposite, top: *Louis Andrews Fischer, "No. 103," water-color costume design for Rex pageant, 1920: "Life's Pilgrimage."*

Opposite, bottom: *Louis Andrews Fischer, "Title Car," water-color float design for Proteus pageant, 1922: "Romance of the Rose."*

*Louis Andrews Fischer, "Moonstone," water-
color costume for Rex pageant, 1930: "The
Jewels of Rex." (The notations on this design
appear to have been made by Léda Plauché, indi-
cating that the costume was used in some later
production.)*

"Coral."

"Pearl."

"Pearl."

*Louis Andrews Fischer, "Tarantella Girl," water-color costume
design for unknown pageant, circa 1930.*

Louis Andrews Fischer, "Columbine," costume design for unknown pageant, circa 1930.

Louis Andrews Fischer, "Pierrot," costume design for unknown pageant, circa 1930.

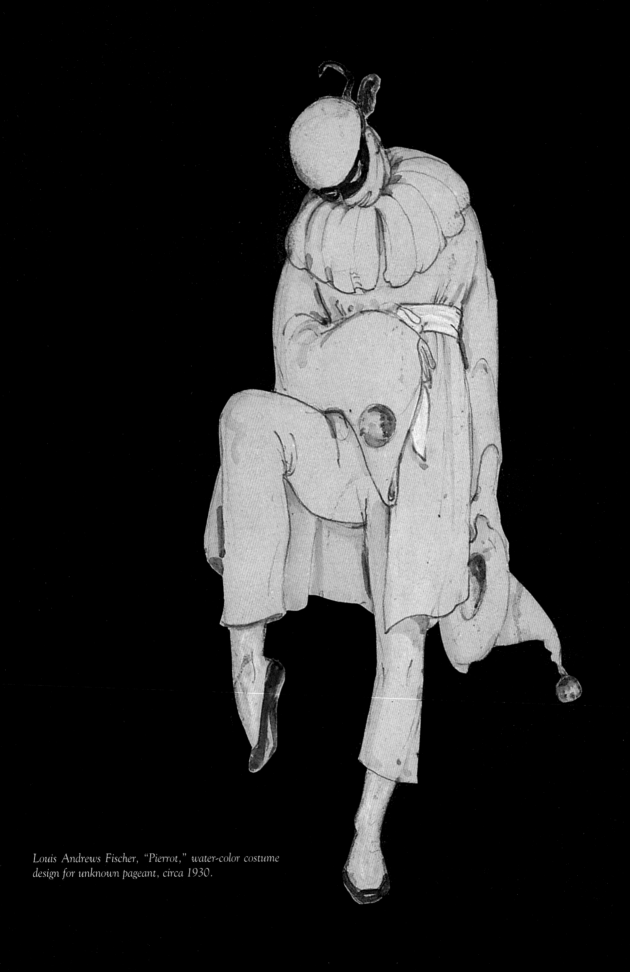

Louis Andrews Fischer, "Pierrot," water-color costume design for unknown pageant, circa 1930.

CHAPTER VI

LÉDA HINCKS PLAUCHÉ

Of all the Carnival designers, none was more steeped in the love of Mardi Gras than Léda Hincks Plauché. Léda Hincks was born in New Orleans on December 30, 1887, into a large wealthy Creole family, and grew up in an Esplanade Avenue mansion where French was still spoken and servants were plentiful. The golden age of old Creole culture was entering its sunset years, but its ancient allegiances to family and Catholicism remained fixed, as did the Creole *joie de vivre* and passion for Mardi Gras. The French Quarter was the longtime home of a number of shops specializing in costumes and masks, and Léda Hincks was quite young when she made her first visits. The colorful array of costumes displayed in shop windows, the musty aisles lined with shelves of eerily waxed masks, with fancifully painted heads of birds and beasts, sparked a lifelong fascination in the Creole child. Years later she would become an important designer of Carnival floats and costumes, and the proprietor of a celebrated shop on Royal Street.

Léda Hincks attended Newcomb College, where she may have worked as one of Wikstrom's student assistants, and graduated in 1907. The following year she married Henry Ovid Plauché, scion of one of the city's grandest Creole families and future president of the New Orleans Cotton Exchange. Altogether unique in the annals of Carnival, the Plauchés formed an extraordinary Mardi Gras couple. He served as captain of the Atlanteans, one of Carnival's smallest and most exclusive organizations, for forty years, and as a member or chairman of the court committees for hundreds of Carnival balls. Mrs. Plauché became the mother of three children and the first artist since Charles Briton to design the parades of the four major societies: Comus, Rex, Momus, and Proteus.

Plauché's earliest designs of record were costumes for the Krewe of Nereus in 1916. The first pageant for which she designed floats and costumes was that of Proteus, in 1923: "Myths and Legends of the North American Indians." The following year brought H. Ryder Haggard's "Neta-Tua," a romance of old Egypt, as Proteus's theme.

During this period, Plauché continued to work as a commercial artist for the Maison Blanche Department Store and served as president of the Women's Advertising Club of New Orleans from 1926 to 1927. Comus turned to her for his 1928 procession, "The Travels of Marco Polo," his first new set of designs since World War I. There was, however, one notable exception—the title car for "Marco Polo" was identical to the title car for Rex in 1909, "The Treasures of the King." Even though Georges Soulie, the great papier-mâché sculptor, had been dead for eight years, the krewes, their designers, and Soulie's son and successor turned to his old molds throughout the 1920s. Such economies, familiar even in the Belle Epoque, were trifles compared to the devastation soon to come.

In early October 1929, guests were summoned to the courtyard of the Patio Royal, where the Plauché's only daughter, Myldred, made her debut to New Orleans society. At the appointed and well-rehearsed hour, the beautiful young debutante, wearing a bright yellow chicken costume designed by her mother, burst through the flimsy shell of a papier-mâché egg to a chorus of cheers. A few weeks later the Jazz Age came to an abrupt halt with the collapse of Wall Street and the beginning of the Great Depression. Preparations for the Carnival of 1930 were already nearing completion by then and continued with few adjustments. It was a triumphant season for the Plauchés. On the Tuesday night before Mardi Gras, Myldred Plauché reigned as queen over the fortieth-anniversary ball of the Atlanteans, and when Proteus appeared the following Monday night, he, too, chose Miss Plauché for his queen. The last Mardi Gras of the Golden Age drew to a close with the Comus parade, "The Legend of Faust" (designed by Léda Plauché) and the meeting of the courts at the Orpheum Theater, in which Myldred appeared once again, as a Rex maid.

When the curtain was raised on the next season, cutbacks were everywhere and they continued to grow. Fewer and fewer people could afford to mask, and floats came to roll with only two or three riders; in 1933, the number of Comus floats was reduced from twenty to seventeen. Momus failed to appear at all for several years, and when he returned in 1937, it was with two fewer floats. Léda Plauché presided as Carnival's designer throughout this period of hardship, but one would never guess that from her beautiful water-color and pen-and-ink drawings. The crisp draftsmanship and delicate color in Plauché's early costume plates recall Alexander, but much of her later work was drenched in the vivid hues of glorious Technicolor. Indeed, around the time that Rex and Momus were added to her drawing board, Plauché received a lucrative offer to design costumes in Hollywood. That, of course, would have meant leaving New Orleans and Creole civilization, and the overture was rejected.

Given the constraints that governed most of her work, what she accomplished in New Orleans was remarkable. Like all of her predecessors, Plauché loved the opulence of Carnival, and in a protracted era of hardship, she contrived to maintain the festival's sense of glamour, its aura of fabulosity. If the papier-mâché figures of the early 1900s rarely appeared, floats were still laden with a profusion of decorative details, and the night parades still rolled through magic seas of ceremonial fire. Among her most important designs of the late 1930s were those for three kings' floats that became Carnival icons: the throne of Proteus rising above the waves in a pink scallop and the golden canopies of Rex and Comus.

Few collections of Plauché's work have survived intact, and the costume designs presented here range from unidentified sketches in the late 1920s to the golden-anniversary ball of the Atlanteans in 1940. These plates were among several hundred watercolors given by Plauché to the New Orleans Public Library in 1959. While most of them are signed—she was the first Carnival artist to do so—the occasional title of a design offers no further clue of krewe name or date, the notable exception being her careful verso labeling of the designs for the Atlanteans in 1940. This ball, one of the greatest

Carnival triumphs of her husband, Henry, included among its wonders a reenactment of the "Destruction of Atlantis" tableaux from the krewe's first ball in 1891. Every character in the tableaux was costumed in gold—golden robes, tunics, and capes—with helmets, hoods, and tiaras also fashioned of the precious metal. Against this backdrop of mythological splendor and familial devotion, the Plauche's daughter, Myldred, was among the former queens of the Atlanteans presented at the ball.

Léda Hincks Plauché, "Insect Fairy," water-color costume design for unknown pageant, circa 1930.

Léda Hincks Plauché, "Insect Fairy," water-color costume design for unknown pageant, circa 1930.

Léda Hincks Plauché, "Persian," water-color costume design for unknown pageant, circa 1928.

Léda Hincks Plauché, "French Nobleman," water-color costume design for unknown pageant, circa 1928.

"Fish."

Léda Hincks Plauché, "Fish," water-color costume design for unknown pageant, circa 1930.

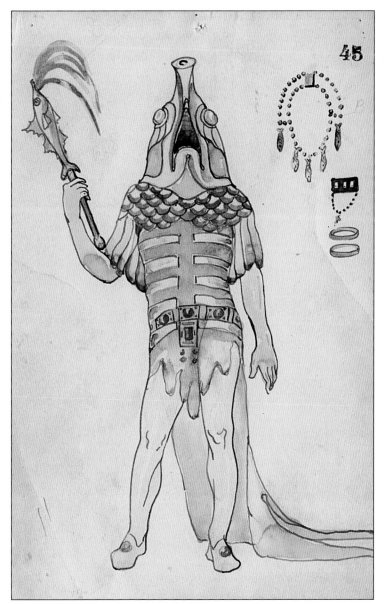

"Fish."

Léda Hincks Plauché, "Balinese Costume,"
unknown pageant, circa 1928.

Léda Hincks Plauché, "Flower Costume,"
unknown pageant, circa 1928.

Léda Hincks Plauché, "Demon," unknown
pageant, circa 1934.

Léda Hincks Plauché, "Queen's Costume,"
unknown pageant, circa 1934.

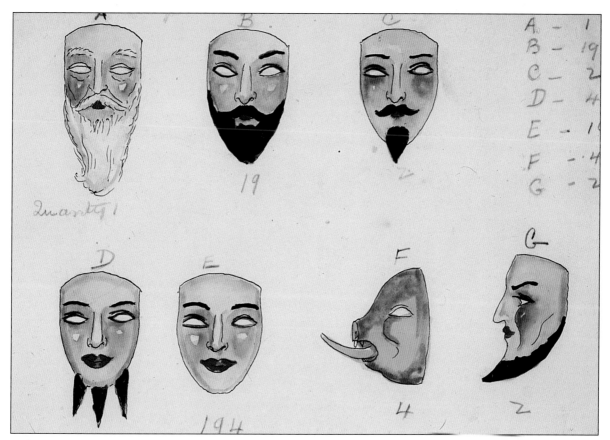

Léda Hincks Plauché, "Masks," ink and water-color designs
for Momus pageant, 1939: "Familiar Proverbs."

Léda Hincks Plauché, "Babylonian Ge-
nie," unknown pageant, circa 1928.

Léda Hincks Plauché, "Lightning Bug,"
unknown pageant, circa 1935.

Léda Hincks Plauché, "South American Indian
Costume," unknown pageant, circa 1935.

Léda Hincks Plauché, "Mardi Gras Golli-Wog,"
unknown pageant, circa 1928.

Léda Hincks Plauché, "Golli-Wog," unknown pageant, circa 1928.

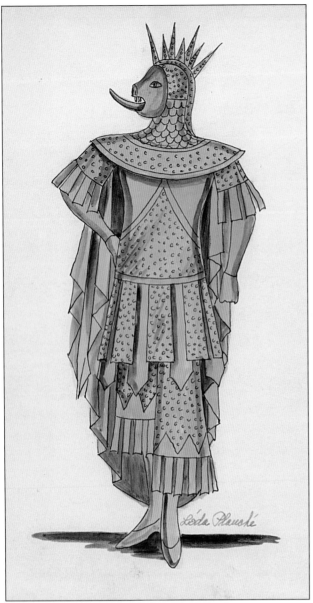

Léda Hincks Plauché, for Atlantean Ball, 1940: "Renascence of Atlantis." (Note the use of a mask pictured on page 151.)

Léda Hincks Plauché, for Atlantean Ball, 1940: "Renascence of Atlantis."

Léda Hincks Plauché, water-color costume design for golden anniversary ball of the Atlanteans, 1940: "Renascence of Atlantis."

Léda Hincks Plauché, for Atlantean Ball, 1940: "Renascence of Atlantis."

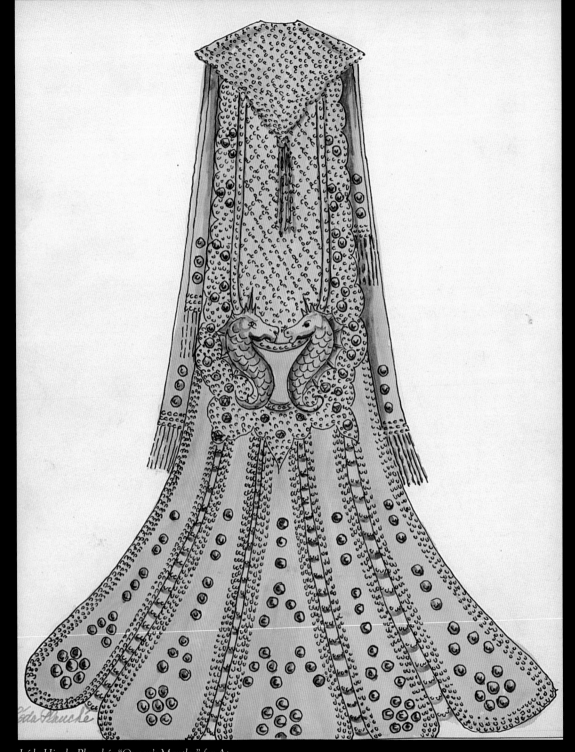

Léda Hincks Plauché, "Queen's Mantle," for At-
lantean Ball, 1940: "Renascence of Atlantis."

King

Silver cloth

Léda Hincks Plauché, "King," for Atlantean Ball,
1940: "Renascence of Atlantis."

INDEX

ACKNOWLEDGMENTS

I would again like to acknowledge the importance of Special Collections, Tulane University, to this project. Of the 277 images in this third volume of *Mardi Gras Treasures*, 220 were drawn from the Tulane archive, and I am grateful to Dr. Wilbur Meneray, director of Special Collections, for his cooperation. I would also like to thank the collection staff members: Mary LeBlanc, Leon Miller, Courtney Page, Carol Hampshire, Kenneth Owen, Ann Case, Dr. Joan Caldwell, and Dr. Robert Sherer.

I am grateful to Priscilla Lawrence, director of The Historic New Orleans Collection, to curator John Magill, and to photographer Jan Brantley for their assistance with the early designs of Charles Briton and the work of Ceneilla Bower Alexander.

I would like to thank Collin Hamer, Irene Wainwright, and Wayne Eberhard of the Louisiana Collection at the New Orleans Public Library for their help with the Wikstrom float plates and Léda Plauché designs. I would also like to thank Marilyn Bordelon for her generosity with her collection.

In the production of this book I would like to acknowledge Rene Vicedomini's scans at Orleans Colour. John Kelly's research assistance was invaluable, as was Jon Newlin's work on the index. At Pelican Publishing, I would like to acknowledge Dr. Milburn Calhoun's ongoing enthusiasm for this project. It has remained a pleasure to work with editor Cynthia Williams, designer Tracey Clements, typsetter Lori Lewis, and secretary Sally Boitnott.

PICTURE CREDITS

17.

86.   88.   90.